HISTORY & GEOGRAPHY 410
OUR WORLD IN REVIEW

Author:
Theresa K. Buskey, B.A., J.D.

Editor:
Alan Christopherson, M.S.

Assistant Editor:
Annette M. Walker, B.S.

Media Credits:
Page 3: © Mike Watson, Moodboard, Thinkstock; **4:** © Stragglist, iStock, Thinkstock; **5:** © Moodboard, Thinkstock; **9:** © Peter Dennis, Thinkstock; © Dorling Kindersley, Thinkstock; © NASA; **10:** © 3DSculptor, iStock, Thinkstock; **13:** © astra490, iStock, Thinkstock; **14:** © Oleg Mitiukhin, iStock, Thinkstock; **15:** © Jupiterimages, Photos.com, Thinkstock; **16:** © Jochen Scheffl, iStock, Thinkstock; **17:** © Comodo777, iStock, Thinkstock; © Hans Ulrich-Ansebach, iStock, Thinkstock; **21:** © Jason Reed, Photodisc, Thinkstock; **23:** © Jack Malipan, iStock, Thinkstock; **25:** © targovcom, iStock, Thinkstock; **27:** © Harry Fox, iStock, Thinkstock; **28:** © Digital Vision, Photodisc, Thinkstock; **31:** © Angel Herrerro de Frutos, iStock, Thinkstock; **32:** © sfinke, iStock, Thinkstock; **33:** © David De Lossey, Valueline, Thinkstock; **37:** © Purestock, Thinkstock; **39:** © StockSolutions, iStock, Thinkstock; **40:** © Robert Cicchetti, iStock, Thinkstock; **44:** © chapsss, iStock, Thinkstock; **45:** © Roman Shiyanov, iStock, Thinkstock; **46:** © Jupiterimages, LiquidLibrary, Thinkstock; **50:** © Jeff Samuels, iStock, Thinkstock; **54:** © Jupiterimages, Creatas, Thinkstock; **55, 57:** © Fuse, Thinkstock; **60:** © Mr Fu, iStock, Thinkstock; **63:** © weltreisenderj, iStock, Thinkstock; **66:** © Stocktrek Images, Thinkstock.

All maps in this book © Image Resources, unless otherwise stated.

Alpha Omega
PUBLICATIONS

804 N. 2nd Ave. E.
Rock Rapids, IA 51246-1759

© MCMXCVIII by Alpha Omega Publications, Inc. All rights reserved.
LIFEPAC is a registered trademark of Alpha Omega Publications, Inc.

All trademarks and/or service marks referenced in this material are the property of their respective owners. Alpha Omega Publications, Inc. makes no claim of ownership to any trademarks and/or service marks other than their own and their affiliates, and makes no claim of affiliation to any companies whose trademarks may be listed in this material, other than their own.

OUR WORLD IN REVIEW

During this year you have learned about deserts, cities, rainforests, mountains, and countries all over the world. This **LIFEPAC**® will review the most important things you have learned this year. At the end of the LIFEPAC you will need to identify the places you have studied on a world map.

The review will be done continent by continent. Each place you have studied on that continent will be reviewed. For the tests, you will need to know the continents, the oceans, and also the geography terms, such as archipelago and peninsula.

Objectives

Read these objectives. The objectives tell you what you will be able to do when you have successfully completed this LIFEPAC. Each section will list according to the numbers below what objectives will be met in that section. When you have finished this LIFEPAC, you should be able to:

1. Describe each of the places you have studied this year in a short statement.
2. Locate each place and feature you have studied on a map and name the continent where it is located.
3. Recognize the meaning of the vocabulary words from throughout the year.
4. Name the continents, oceans, equator, Tropics of Cancer and Capricorn, and the North and South Poles.

1. EUROPE AND THE EXPLORERS

The people of Europe were the first ones to fully explore and map our world. Much of the work they did was during the Age of Exploration, from the 1400s into the 1700s. Antarctica, the last place explored on earth, was not completely mapped until the 1950s.

The Europeans set up many of the map lines and place names that we use today. Thanks to their work and modern means of exploration, we know a great deal about the different places on our planet. You will review some of these explorers and their work.

You studied several places in Europe this year. You studied the mountain country of Switzerland, the grassland country of Ukraine, and the island country of Iceland. You also studied the cities of London and Istanbul. Istanbul is in both Europe and Asia. Because it is in the country of Turkey, which is mainly in Asia, Istanbul will be reviewed with that continent.

Objectives

Review these objectives. When you have completed this section, you should be able to:

1. Describe each of the places you have studied this year in a short statement.
2. Locate each place and feature you have studied on a map and name the continent where it is located.
3. Recognize the meaning of the vocabulary words from the year.
4. Name the continents, oceans, equator, Tropics of Cancer and Capricorn, and the North and South Poles.

Vocabulary

All of the vocabulary in this LIFEPAC is review. Old vocabulary words will be in bold print the first time they are used. Any words you do not recognize, you should look up in the dictionary. You will be tested on these words.

Geography and Exploration

Maps. The best map of the earth is a **globe**. It is the same shape as the earth, a **sphere**. Any flat map, like the one on the following page, makes parts of the earth look the wrong size or difficult to see, but flat maps can be used to find places and features. Use the map to review some of the features and map lines on our earth.

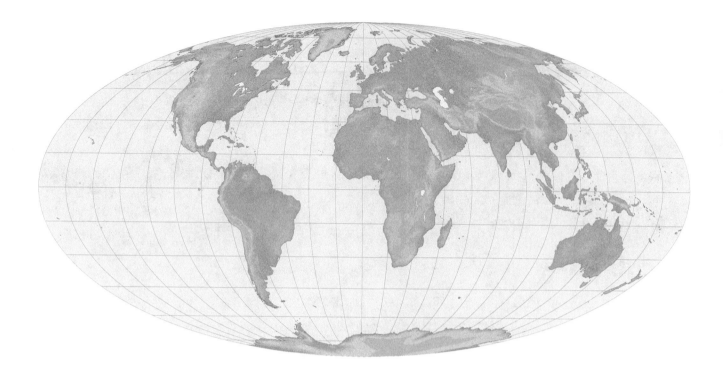

| A view of our world

 Map work. Use an atlas or encyclopedia, but first see how many you can find without any help.

1.1   Label these: the four **oceans**, seven **continents**, **equator**, **Tropics of Cancer** and **Capricorn**.

1.2   Put a circle around the **archipelagoes** of the West Indies and Japan.

1.3   Put an "X" on the islands of Greenland and Madagascar.

1.4   Put a "G" on the **Gulf** of Mexico and a "B" on Hudson **Bay**.

1.5   Put a square around the **Isthmus** of Panama and Suez.

1.6   Draw an arrow through the **Strait** of Gibraltar and the Denmark Strait.

1.7   Put an "S" on the Mediterranean and Caribbean **Seas**.

1.8   Put an "L" on the Great **Lakes** and Lake Victoria.

1.9   Put a "P" on the Arabian **Peninsula** and Baja California.

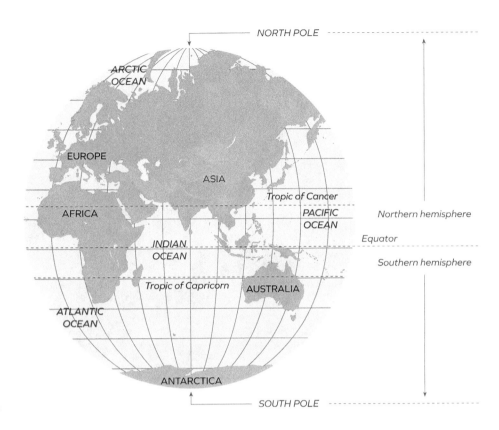

| Eastern Hemisphere

Geography. The equator is the imaginary line that runs around the middle of the earth. The half of the earth north of the equator is called the Northern **Hemisphere** ("hemi" means half), while the half to the south is the Southern Hemisphere. The Eastern Hemisphere is Asia, Africa, Europe and Australia. The Americas are the Western Hemisphere.

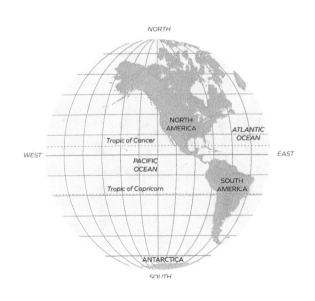

| Western Hemisphere

At the very top of the earth, as far north as you can go is the North Pole. It is in the middle of a frozen ocean. The South Pole is at the bottom of the world, on the continent of Antarctica. The areas around the Poles, the **polar regions**, are the coldest places on earth. On the other hand, the area around the equator is the hottest place on earth. Most of the time it gets warmer as you move toward the equator and colder as you move toward the Poles. You can make a good guess about how cold a place is by looking at how far it is from the equator.

Match these items.

1.10 _____ Eastern Hemisphere

1.11 _____ Western Hemisphere

1.12 _____ South Pole

1.13 _____ peninsula

1.14 _____ strait

1.15 _____ isthmus

1.16 _____ sea

1.17 _____ archipelago

a. land bridge between bigger pieces of land

b. land with water on three sides

c. as far south as you can go on earth

d. Africa, Asia, and Europe

e. North and South America

f. narrow waterway that joins two larger bodies of water

g. a group of islands

h. part of an ocean all or partly surrounded by land

Early Exploration. Europeans in the 1400s loved spices. They could be used to keep food from spoiling and make it taste better. Most spices came from Asia and were very expensive. They had to come to Europe by long, dangerous sea and land **routes**. Several brave European explorers decided to find an all-water route to Asia that would be safer and faster. These men began to explore the world beyond Europe in their search for spices.

Prince Henry the Navigator was a famous explorer who led the way in searching for a water route to Asia. Prince Henry started a school in his country of Portugal to teach sailors about **navigation**. Under his leadership, Portuguese ships began to explore farther and farther down the coast of Africa. The Portuguese reached the southern end of that continent in 1488 and sailed a fleet around Africa to India in 1497. Prince Henry had died years before that, but it was his dream and planning that made it possible.

Another explorer, Christopher Columbus, tried to find a route to Asia by sailing west from Europe for the country of Spain. Instead, he discovered the Americas in 1492.

He always thought he was near India on all of his four trips to the "New World," as it became known. The islands where he first landed are called the West Indies because of his mistake.

| Columbus' ships, the Niña, the Pinta, and the Santa Maria

Other explorers eventually realized that the Americas were not Asia. Another man set out to find out just how big the world is. Ferdinand Magellan sailed from Spain in 1519 with five ships, intending to go all the way around the world. It was a very difficult journey. Magellan did not know how huge the Pacific Ocean was. Magellan was killed in the Philippine Islands after finally reaching Asia. Only one of his ships and eighteen men made the first successful trip around the world.

Modern Exploration. In the modern explorations of the world, men have been able to go under the ocean and into space. Beginning in the 1800s people used diving suits attached to an air hose above the water to explore the ocean. Jacques Cousteau invented the aqualung in 1943, which allowed divers the freedom to move around under the water without a hose.

In deeper oceans, where men could not live, special boats that were completely sealed were used to explore. The first such ship was the bathysphere, a hollow steel ball with windows that was lowered into the depths by a wire cable. Later diving ships had their own air and could move around. In 1960, a deep water ship, called the *Trieste* went into the Mariana **Trench**, the deepest place in the world.

Rockets were first used to explore space after World War II (1938-45). *Sputnik*, from the Soviet Union, was the first man-made **satellite** ever put into space. It was launched in 1957. After that the United States and the Soviet Union raced to build new ships to explore space. The Soviets won many of the early successes: first man in space, first woman in space, and the first space walk.

| *Sputnik*

The American space program was led by NASA (National Aeronautic and Space Administration). It has gone through five stages. Mercury, the first stage, carried one man into space at a time. Under Mercury, in 1961, Alan Shepard was the first American in space, and John Glenn was the first American to orbit the earth in 1962.

The Gemini program began in 1965 and put two men at a time into space. Apollo, which carried three men into space, was launched in 1968. Under the Apollo program, Neil Armstrong became the first man to walk on the moon. Several other Apollo ships went to the moon after that. The last Apollo mission, in 1975, was a link-up between an American and a Soviet space ship. It showed that the two countries could work together in space.

Skylab was a small space station in orbit around the earth. Beginning in 1973, it was used by three crews to do experiments in space and learn about how people can live in space. It fell out of earth's orbit in 1979.

The Space Shuttle, the fifth stage of the American space program, was first launched in 1981. It could carry five to seven people and was the first reusable spaceship. It landed on a runway like an airplane, instead of splashing down into the ocean like earlier ships. Space shuttles made over one hundred thirty trips to launch satellites, repair satellites, and do experiments in space. The satellites which the Shuttle launched are used to watch the weather on earth, allow people to communicate, and explore the rest of the universe. So, modern man continues to explore just as Columbus and Magellan did.

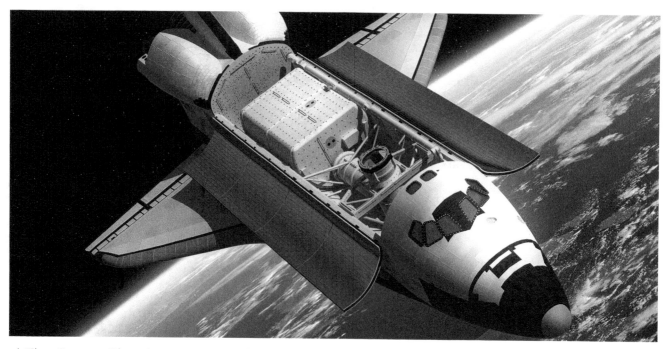

| The Space Shuttle was reusable and could land like an airplane.

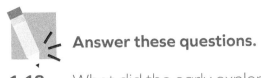

Answer these questions.

1.18 What did the early explorers want from Asia? _____

1.19 For what country did Columbus and Magellan sail? _____

1.20 How did divers in the 1800s get air while under the water?

_____

1.21 What country put the first man and woman in space? _____

1.22 What stage of the American space program put a man on the moon?

_____

1.23 What was new and unusual about the Space Shuttle ships?

_____

Match these items.

1.24 _____ Prince Henry

1.25 _____ Columbus

1.26 _____ Magellan

1.27 _____ *Sputnik*

1.28 _____ *Trieste*

1.29 _____ Cousteau

1.30 _____ Mercury

1.31 _____ Alan Shepard

1.32 _____ Neil Armstrong

1.33 _____ Skylab

a. first satellite in space

b. explored the Mariana Trench

c. planned to sail around Africa

d. first stage of U.S. space program

e. first man to walk on the moon

f. led the first trip around the world

g. first American in space

h. discovered America while looking for Asia

i. American space station

j. invented the aqualung

| Europe

Map work.

1.34 Most of the southern border of Europe is the _____ Sea.

1.35 The land of Europe is divided from Asia by the _____ Mountains in the east.

1.36 The Strait of Gibraltar connects the _____ Sea with the _____ Ocean.

1.37 Circle the capitals of Britain, Ukraine, Switzerland, and Iceland.

Review of Europe

Switzerland. Switzerland is a small, freedom-loving, landlocked country in the mountains of central Europe. The largest mountain range in Europe, the Alps, covers the southern part of the country. Most of the people live on the Swiss **Plateau**, between the Alps in the south and the Jura Mountains in the north. The plateau has many beautiful lakes, including Lake Constance and Lake Geneva. The land has few natural resources except for its fast-moving streams. The Swiss people use the rivers to make **hydroelectric** power to run their factories and homes.

| Swiss milk and chocolate

Switzerland is divided into cantons that are similar to states in America. Three of the cantons created the country when they rebelled against Austria in 1291. The Swiss people fought hard for their independence and became famous as soldiers all over Europe; but eventually the Swiss decided they did not want to fight in the wars of Europe. They have stayed **neutral** for about 500 years! Many international groups are in Switzerland because it is neutral. The best known is the Red Cross, which helps people in need world-wide.

Switzerland is a very wealthy country despite its lack of resources. The people must bring in resources from other countries, build a product, and then sell it. Things made in Switzerland are very expensive. People still buy them, though, because they are so well made. Swiss watches, in particular, are known all over the world for how well they work.

Switzerland is also known for its delicious cheese and chocolate. Because Switzerland is neutral and has strict laws, many people feel safe putting their money in Swiss banks. That is another source of the country's riches. Still another is the Alps, which many people come to visit every year. Thus Switzerland has by hard work, good government, and cleverness, made itself into a wealthy country.

Ukraine. Ukraine is called the "Breadbasket of Europe." It is the second-largest country in Europe, located in east Europe, north of the Black Sea. Most of the country is covered with **fertile** grasslands called the steppes. Sugar beets, grain, and cattle are all raised on the rich land. The country is also rich in **mineral** resources.

Ukraine has been ruled by many different countries, including Poland and Russia. It was independent for a short time in the 1600s under the Cossacks, the **peasant** soldiers of Ukraine, and again briefly in 1917. Until 1991, Ukraine was ruled by **communists** from Russia under the Union of Soviet Socialist Republics (USSR), a country that forced many "republics" such as Ukraine to join it.

| A Cossack soldier

Ukraine was never able to become a rich country through its resources because of its communist government. The communists ran all the farms and businesses. They were **corrupt** and did a bad job. Finally, in 1991, the USSR fell apart and Ukraine became independent.

The people of the Ukraine are Slavs, who usually are part of the Eastern Orthodox Church. They are famous for their decorated Easter eggs and their **embroidery**. It has been difficult for them to change to a independent government that is no longer communist. They must learn new ways to use the richness of their land.

Complete these sentences.

1.38 The mountains of Switzerland are the _____ and the _____ .

1.39 Lake _____ and Lake _____ are two of the lakes on the Swiss Plateau.

1.40 The Red Cross has its headquarters in Switzerland because the country is

_____ .

1.41 Comparing Ukraine and Switzerland, _____ has more resources, but _____ is richer.

1.42   Switzerland is famous for its _____ , _____ , and

_____ .

1.43   Ukraine is called the "_____ of Europe" because of its fertile

grasslands called the _____ .

1.44   Ukraine's peasant soldiers were called _____ .

1.45   In 1991 Ukraine became independent from the _____ and no longer

has a _____ government.

1.46   The people of the Ukraine usually belong to the _____

_____ Church.

London. London is a **port** city on the Thames **River** in the United Kingdom on the British Isles, north of France. The city was founded by the Romans in the year A.D. 13. It became the capital of Britain (the United Kingdom), home of the British **monarch**, and center of the British Empire, which ruled over colonies all over the world in the 1800s.

The City (spelled with a capital "C") is the oldest part of London, that which was once within the walls built by the Romans. It is one square mile in size, while the rest of London covers about 600 square miles. A person born within the sound of the bells of a certain church in the City, St. Mary-le-Bow, is called a Cockney.

| Buckingham Palace, the queen's home

Many historic places are in London, including the Tower of London (famous as a prison), St. Paul's Cathedral, Trafalgar Square (honoring a British naval hero), and Buckingham Palace (the monarch's home). Many important ceremonies such as the Trooping of the Colour, which honors the day the queen was crowned, and the opening of Parliament, the first day of a new government year, are celebrated in London.

London is the largest city in Britain and the home of the government. The British parliament, or Congress, meets at Westminster Palace in London, and the head of the government, the Prime Minister, lives at Number 10 Downing Street.

Early London became an important city as a port. Today the ships stop further down the Thames and never reach the city, but it is still the most important city in Great Britain.

Iceland. Iceland is an island nation north and west of Europe. Its nearest neighbor is Greenland in North America across the Denmark Strait. It has only a little arable land, along the **coast** where most of the people live. The land is good only for a few **crops** that grow well in the cold and for raising **livestock** such as sheep. The interior of the island is wild and few people live there.

There are several **glaciers** and many **volcanoes** on the island. In fact, the volcanoes heat water under the earth, creating hot springs and geysers. The people of Iceland use these hot waters to heat their homes and businesses. Geothermal energy and hydroelectric power from the fast-moving rivers give Iceland power without causing **pollution**. The skies and water of the country are much clearer than most developed (modern) countries.

| Eyjafjallajökull Volcano in Iceland

The clean water helps the fishing industry, which is the main source of income in the country. Icelanders manufacture some goods for their own use, but it is mostly fish or wool products that they export.

Iceland was settled by Vikings, fierce warriors from Europe, in A.D. 874. The Vikings started the world's oldest parliament, the *Althing*, on this island in A.D. 930. Many sagas, or stories, were written about the wild Vikings and how they settled the island.

| Iceland was first settled by Vikings.

| A Viking Runestone

The people of Iceland were able to read and write these sagas even when few people in the rest of Europe could read or write.

Beginning in 1264, Iceland was taken over first by Norway and then by Denmark. Denmark made the Icelanders very poor by allowing the merchants who traded with the people to cheat them. The islanders also suffered when disease and volcanoes killed thousands. Gradually Denmark gave Iceland more freedom, and it became an independent country in 1944.

The people of Iceland speak and write a Norse language that has changed very little since the Vikings. Children can read the old sagas in school that were written 700 years ago. Icelanders still love to read and write. They publish more books per person than any other country on earth! Their harsh history did not dim their love of learning.

Put an *L* if the statement is about London or an *I* if it is about Iceland.

1.47	_____	founded by the Romans
1.48	_____	the City covers only one square mile
1.49	_____	the *Althing*
1.50	_____	British government
1.51	_____	glaciers and volcanoes
1.52	_____	little pollution due to geothermal, hydroelectric power
1.53	_____	publishes the most books per person in the world
1.54	_____	founded in A.D. 13
1.55	_____	founded in A.D. 874
1.56	_____	Buckingham Palace, Trafalgar Square
1.57	_____	Thames River
1.58	_____	settled by Vikings
1.59	_____	exports mainly fish and wool
1.60	_____	ruled by Denmark until 1944
1.61	_____	Cockney is within the sounds of St. Mary-le-Bow's bells
1.62	_____	most people live near the coast, not the interior
1.63	_____	Norse language, has changed very little in hundreds of years

Review the material in this section to prepare for the Self Test. The Self Test will check your understanding of this section. Any items you miss on this test will show you what areas you will need to restudy in order to prepare for the unit test.

SELF TEST 1

Choose the correct vocabulary word from the list (2 points each answer).

archipelago	fertile	strait	landlocked	neutral
globe	isthmus	plateau	peasant	communism

1.01 _____ a group of islands

1.02 _____ a model of the earth

1.03 _____ a working-class farmer in Europe

1.04 _____ a plain in the mountains or high above sea level

1.05 _____ a narrow bridge of land connecting two larger pieces of land

1.06 _____ on neither side in a quarrel or war

1.07 _____ able to produce much; producing crops easily

1.08 _____ surrounded by land

1.09 _____ a system in which all or most property is owned by the state

1.010 _____ a narrow waterway that connects two larger bodies of water

Each statement is about a European city or country. Choose the correct one using an _L_ for London, _I_ for Iceland, _S_ for Switzerland, and _U_ for Ukraine (4 points each answer).

1.011 _____ Alps and Jura Mountains

1.012 _____ the steppes

1.013 _____ home of the British monarch

1.014 _____ port on the Thames River

1.015 _____ first cantons became independent of Austria in 1291

1.016 _____ settled by Vikings

1.017 _____ run by communists until 1991

1.018 _____ main religion is Eastern Orthodox

1.019 _____ Bern is the capital

1.020 _____ people live along the coast, not the interior; many volcanoes and glaciers

Match these items (3 points each answer).

1.021	_____	Western Hemisphere	a.	first satellite in space
1.022	_____	Prince Henry	b.	reusable American spaceship
1.023	_____	*Sputnik*	c.	American space program that went to the moon
1.024	_____	Apollo		
1.025	_____	Magellan	d.	sailed west from Europe and found the West Indies
1.026	_____	Columbus	e.	led first trip around the world
1.027	_____	Space Shuttle	f.	first man to walk on the moon
1.028	_____	Neil Armstrong	g.	planned route around Africa
1.029	_____	Skylab	h.	American space station
1.030	_____	Eastern Hemisphere	i.	Africa, Asia, Europe
			j.	North and South America

Write *true* or *false* on the blank (each answer 2 points).

1.031 _____ The Tropic of Cancer is north of the equator.

1.032 _____ The North Pole is on Antarctica.

1.033 _____ The first man in space was an American.

1.034 _____ The explorers wanted to find a water route to Asia to get aluminum and gold.

1.035 _____ The *Trieste* explored the deepest part of the ocean, the Mariana Trench.

✓ **Teacher check:**

Score _____

Initials _____

Date _____

80 / 100

2. ASIA AND AFRICA

Asia is the largest continent on earth. This section will review several Asian places, including the seaport cities of Istanbul and Hong Kong, the Arabian and Gobi Deserts, the mountain country of Nepal, and the island nation of Japan.

Africa is connected to Asia by the Isthmus of Suez, which is divided by the Suez Canal. In Africa you will review the Kalahari Desert as well as the Sahara Desert, the largest desert in the world. This section will also cover the rainforest country of the Congo and the grassland country of Kenya.

Objectives

Review these objectives. When you have completed this section, you should be able to:

1. Describe each of the places you have studied this year in a short statement.
2. Locate each place and feature you have studied on a map and name the continent where it is located.
3. Recognize the meaning of the vocabulary words from throughout the year.
4. Name and locate the continents, oceans, equator, Tropics of Cancer and Capricorn, and the North and South Poles.

Review of Asia

Asia and Europe are separated by a imaginary line drawn along the Ural Mountains, the Caspian Sea, the Caucasus Mountains, and the Black Sea. The land of the two continents is often called Eurasia because the line between them is imaginary.

Istanbul is a city that is right on the dividing line between Europe and Asia. It has a long history tied to both lands. South of Istanbul is the Arabian Peninsula and the desert that fills it. East of Arabia, in the tall Himalaya Mountains, is the small country of Nepal. Behind the Himalaya's rain shadow, to the north, is the Gobi Desert. South of the Gobi, on the coast of China, is the former British colony of Hong Kong and its former capital, Victoria. Finally, north of Hong Kong in the Pacific Ocean is the island nation of Japan, "the source of the sun." This year you have crossed Asia from Istanbul in the west to Japan in the east.

| Asia

 Map work.

2.1   Trace over the line between Europe and Asia.

2.2   The Gobi Desert is mostly in what two countries?

2.3   What is the big country in the center of the Arabian Desert?

_____

2.4   Circle Istanbul, Victoria, Nepal, and Japan on the map.

2.5   Name the capitals of Nepal and Japan.

_____

Istanbul. Istanbul is built on two peninsulas on either side of the Bosporus Strait between the Mediterranean and Black Seas. The west side is Europe, and the east is Asia. The European side, built on an **estuary**, was the **ancient** city and still has the **ruins** of the city wall. The wall surrounded the city and a chain blocked the **harbor**, making it very difficult to attack.

The European side was founded as a Greek city called Byzantium, before Jesus was born. It was rebuilt by the Roman emperor Constantine in A.D. 330, and it became his capital, Constantinople. It was the capital of the Eastern Roman Empire, the Byzantine Empire, for almost a thousand years. Finally, in 1453 the Ottoman Turks captured the city and made it the capital of their own empire. They renamed the city Istanbul, but their empire slowly grew smaller until, today, only the country of Turkey is left of it.

The people of Istanbul are Turkish Muslims, but they are not as careful about that religion's many rules as are some other Muslim countries. They worship in buildings called mosques. One of the most famous mosques in Istanbul is Hagia Sophia. It was built by Constantine as a Christian church. It was rebuilt by a later emperor named Justinian, then under the Ottomans it was turned into a mosque. Many other Roman, Byzantine, and Ottoman buildings can be seen in this historic city.

| Hagia Sophia

Hong Kong. Hong Kong was a colony of Great Britain from 1841 until 1997. The British forced China to give them the harbor to use to trade opium, an **addictive** drug. Over the years China became a cruel, communist country. Many **refugees** fled from China to freedom in Hong Kong, making it one of the most crowded places on earth. China agreed not to change Hong Kong's way of life for fifty years when they took the colony back in 1997.

Hong Kong has a huge harbor that is open to the ocean in two places, because it is behind Hong Kong Island. Victoria, the former capital, is on the island. Kowloon is the harbor city on the **mainland**. The New Territories is the farmland that spreads out around Kowloon. Most of the people live in the two cities, and space is extremely limited.

The hard working Chinese people there have made Hong Kong a place to buy all kinds of things like clothes, carvings, jewelry, and art. People come from all over the world to shop in Hong Kong. The visitors also come to enjoy the great food of the city. Everything is freshly made, and the people expect the best.

Very few of the Chinese people of Hong Kong are Christians. Most follow the Chinese religion which is a mix of Confucianism, Taoism, and Buddhism. Mainly the people believe in good or bad luck. They go to *feng shui* men who tell them what to do to be lucky.

Put an *I* beside the statements about Istanbul and an *H* beside those about Hong Kong.

2.6	_____	British colony
2.7	_____	Byzantium, Constantinople
2.8	_____	Bosporus Strait
2.9	_____	Victoria, Kowloon, New Territories
2.10	_____	religion a mix of Confucianism, Taoism, Buddhism
2.11	_____	religion is Muslim
2.12	_____	in Europe and Asia
2.13	_____	Chinese people
2.14	_____	famous for its shopping and food, not its history
2.15	_____	Hagia Sophia
2.16	_____	capital of Byzantine and Ottoman Empires

Arabian Desert. The Arabian Desert is the name for all of the deserts on the Arabian peninsula. The desert names are Arabic, like Rub' al-Khali (empty quarter). It is near the area of low rainfall along the Tropic of Cancer, and **moisture** is blocked by mountains along the east coast of the peninsula. The desert land has large amounts of oil, which has made most of the countries there rich.

The people of this desert used to be **nomads** who herded sheep, goats, camels, and horses between **oases**. They used their camels, the "ships of the desert," to trade across their dry land. They would trade meat, wool, and hides for jewelry, crops, and weapons. They thought it was important to be kind to visitors, but they also fought fierce battles with their enemies. This desert was the place where the Muslim religion began in the A.D. 600s, and most of the nomads accepted it.

| Camels are "ships of the desert"

Gobi Desert. The Gobi Desert is in Mongolia and northern China. It is a cold, northern desert in the rain shadow of the Himalayas. It is surrounded by mountains on three sides. There are no oases there, and rivers coming out of the mountains dry up quickly. People must dig wells to reach underground water. The center of the desert is **barren**, stony ground, but there are dry steppes around the edges.

Mongol nomads have raised **livestock** on the steppes for many, many years, and some still do. They were very good horsemen, who could ride and shoot at the same time. The Mongols could not trade with anyone, so they lived on the milk and meat of their animals. Their houses were a felt (packed wool) covering spread over a fold-out frame. Called a *yurt* or *ger*, it was good protection against the cold, dry winds of the Gobi.

Complete these sentences.

2.17   One of the Arabic names for the Arabian Deserts is the _____ .

2.18   The Arabian countries have become rich from the _____ under their desert.

2.19   The _____ religion began on the Arabian Peninsula in the A.D. 600s.

2.20   Arabian nomads used _____ to trade across the desert.

2.21   The Gobi Desert is in _____ and China in the rain shadow of
             the _____ Mountains.

2.22   There are _____ where livestock can be raised around the
             edges of the Gobi.

2.23   A Mongol nomad's home is called a _____ .

Nepal. Nepal, one of the poorest countries in the world is located in the world's highest
mountains, the Himalayas. It is between China and India. Its land is divided into three
parts: the rainforests below the mountains, the **heartland** in the lower mountains
and valleys, and the high Himalayan peaks. Many visitors come to climb or "trek" the
mountain trails. Tourism is the country's main source of money.

Nepal began in the Kathmandu Valley in the center of the country. Many different
kings and **dynasties** ruled from there. The rulers tried to keep the Europeans, who had
conquered India and **overwhelmed** China, out of their country. Very few people were
allowed to visit the country before 1950. A change in the government in 1950 meant
people could finally come to explore and map. The country is still ruled by a king.

The people of Nepal are from many different tribes. Religious festivals and art are very
important to them. Most Nepali follow the Hindu religion, which came from India. Some
follow Buddhism, which also came from India. For many years it was illegal to teach
about Christ in Nepal but since 2008 the door has been open to evangelism.

Most of Nepal has no roads. Only trails lead up to the villages in the mountains. That
is true around Mount Everest, the tallest mountain on earth. Everything mountain

climbers or anyone else needs must be brought in by **porters** or on yaks. The Sherpa people who live near Everest are famous as mountain guides and porters. But, Nepal has few resources except its high mountains, and few industries to make money for its people or to build roads.

Japan. Japan is an archipelago nation just east of Korea off the coast of Asia. Japan has four main islands and almost 4,000 smaller ones. Honshu (largest and the Japanese homeland), Hokkaido, Kyushu, and Shikoku are the main islands. The Japanese islands are the tops of a chain of underwater mountains. There are many

| A Sherpa carrying supplies

volcanoes and earthquakes there. Most of the people live on the east side of the islands, where the ocean currents warm the land. The west coast, toward Asia, is cooled by currents from the north, and fewer people live there.

Japan is a very old country. The current emperor is from the Yamato **clan**, which began to rule the country 1500 years ago. During most of Japanese history, the emperor had no power. The *shogun*, or general, ruled the country in the emperor's name. Japan was never conquered by the Europeans, but in 1853, they were forced by Commodore Matthew Perry of the U.S. to allow trade. The Japanese then began to make their country modern to protect it.

The rebuilt Japanese army began to conquer parts of Asia in the 1900s. During World War II, the country conquered most of southeast Asia and attacked Hawaii, which brought the U.S. into the war. Japan was defeated and **occupied** by the American army. The hard-working Japanese people rebuilt their cities and factories. Today, Japan is a modern, wealthy nation.

In spite of the wealth of the country, people live in small homes. Japan is very crowded, and land for houses is expensive. People work hard and are taught to be very polite. Children must study long hours and even go to special schools in the afternoon so they can get into the best colleges to get a good job. People are expected to work together, not be independent, in Japan.

Much of the Japanese culture (writing, art, religion, music) is taken from China. The main religion is Shinto, which worships gods of nature. The Japanese people love nature and art about nature. Paintings and gardens are popular. All kinds of beautiful things are honored by the Japanese. Everyone is expected to write poetry and form their letters beautifully when they write. Japan is a crowded place where beauty is found in little things and small places.

| The tea ceremony is very important in Japanese society.

Put an *N* if the statement is about Nepal or a *J* if it is about Japan.

2.24 _____ one of the poorest countries in the world

2.25 _____ an archipelago

2.26 _____ emperor is from the Yamato clan

2.27 _____ main religion is Shinto

2.28 _____ main religion is Hinduism

2.29 _____ Mount Everest, world's tallest mountain

2.30 _____ Honshu, Hokkaido, Kyushu, and Shikoku

2.31 _____ volcanoes and earthquakes

2.32 _____ between India and China

2.33 _____ Himalaya Mountains

Review of Africa

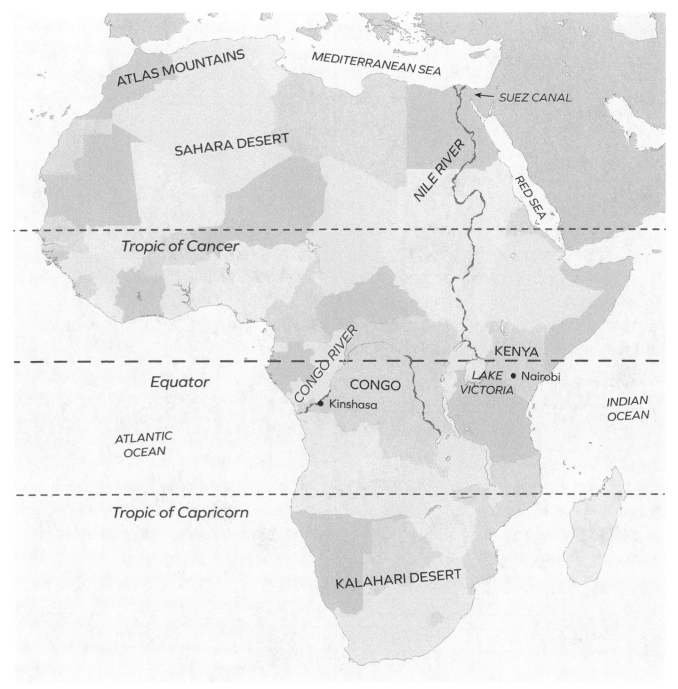

| Africa

 Map work.

2.34   What map line runs through the Sahara Desert? _____

2.35   What map line runs through the Kalahari Desert?

_____

2.36   What map line runs through Kenya? _____

2.37   Put an "X" on the **mouths** of the Nile and Congo Rivers.

2.38   Circle the Democratic Republic of the Congo, Kenya, and the Suez Canal.

2.39   Name the capitals of Congo and Kenya. _____

Africa is the second-largest continent. Because the equator goes through it, most African countries are in the **tropics**. It is connected to Asia by the Isthmus of Suez. The Suez Canal crosses the isthmus to connect the Red and Mediterranean Seas. The world's longest river, the Nile, and second-largest lake, Victoria, are both on this continent. This year you studied two countries, Kenya and Congo, in the center of Africa, and two deserts, the Sahara and Kalahari, at either end.

Sahara Desert. The Sahara is the largest desert in the world. It covers most of North Africa along the Tropic of Cancer (areas along the two tropic lines are often dry). Moisture is blocked from reaching the Sahara by the Atlas Mountains. The desert is growing larger, and the dry area along its southern edge is called the **Sahel**.

The Sahara nomads were very much like the nomads of the Arabian Desert. They herded livestock from one oasis to another and traded for goods their animals could not give them. These people also became Muslims when that religion reached North Africa in the A.D. 700s.

Caravans of camels carried on important trade across the Sahara in ancient times. The tropical forests of central Africa needed salt and had gold to trade for it. The trading of salt from the north for gold from the south made several African empires rich before the Europeans came. Much of the trade went through the city of Timbuktu, which is now in the country of Mali, so even the world's largest desert was not completely empty.

Kalahari Desert. The Kalahari Desert is mainly in the country of Botswana on the Tropic of Capricorn. It is a bowl-shaped desert located up in the mountains that block moisture from reaching it on three sides. It gets more rain than most deserts, but there is very little water above ground. The rain that does fall collects in pans, large flat areas, for animals and people to use until it dries up.

The Bushmen of the Kalahari were hunter/gatherers. They hunted for meat and gathered the food of the desert to eat. They did not keep animals. They moved from place to place to find food and water. They owned very few things because they had to carry everything themselves. Very few people still live this way anywhere in the world.

| Bushmen setting a trap

 Put the correct word on the blank.

2.40 _____ second-largest continent

2.41 _____ isthmus that connects Asia and Africa

2.42 _____ longest river in the world

2.43 _____ second-largest lake in the world

2.44 _____ largest desert in the world

2.45 _____ dry area along southern edge of Sahara

2.46 _____ religion of the Sahara nomads

2.47 _____ two items traded by camel across the Sahara

2.48 _____ trade city of the Sahara

2.49 _____ country of the Kalahari Desert

2.50 _____ African desert on the Tropic of Capricorn

2.51 _____ Kalahari rain collects in these

2.52 _____ Bushmen were this type of people (how they got their food)

Congo and the Congo River. The Congo River, one of the world's largest rivers is in the middle of a tropical rainforest. The river crosses the equator twice on its route. **Rapids** block ocean ships from trading on the river, but it is **navigable** by riverboats between the rapids. These riverboats allow people along the river to trade jungle crops and products for city goods carried by the merchants on the boats.

Most of the Congo River is in the country of the Democratic Republic of the Congo (Congo). An ancient kingdom called Kongo was at the mouth of the river when the Portuguese arrived looking for a way around Africa in the 1480s. The Portuguese destroyed the kingdom by taking slaves from the region. The river and its tributaries were finally explored and mapped by Henry Stanley in the late 1800s. The king of Belgium, who hired Stanley, claimed all of the country as his own personal property in 1885. Almost all of Africa was taken over by European countries in the late 1800s.

The people of the Congo region were treated very badly by Belgium and its king. The country finally became independent in 1960, and a **civil war** broke out. Joseph Mobutu took over the country as a **dictator** in 1965. He and his friends robbed the country of everything they could, leaving the people unbelievably poor by the time he was overthrown in 1997. The country was so poor that usually only schools and hospitals run by Christian groups were still working.

The people of the Congo come from many different tribes and often fight with each other. They did not agree to create a country, the Belgians just put them together in one. Most of the people live by farming a small piece of land and hunting or fishing.

| The Congo River

Many of the animals of the Congo rainforest are in danger of being hunted until there are none left, but the poor people are hungry or need the money they can get from animal products. However, the Congo rainforest is not being destroyed, because the people do not have the money to do it.

| People on safari watching an elephant

Kenya. Kenya is also on the equator, but it is mainly savanna, not rainforest. Savanna is tropical grassland that has a wet and dry season, but little change in temperature. Kenya's savanna is not good cropland. In fact, the best land for crops in Kenya is in the mountains in the southwest. The dry savanna is home mostly to wild animals and is used to raise cattle.

Kenya is famous for its wild animals. People come from all over the world on **safari** to see lions, elephants, antelope, giraffes, and leopards. The animals are protected in huge national parks. Only coffee and tea crops bring in more money than tourism for Kenya.

Some of the cities on Kenya's east coast were once part of a group of **city-states** that traded with Greece, Rome, and the Arabs during the centuries before the Europeans conquered Africa. The Bantu people of these cities mixed with the Arabs to create the Swahili culture and language (one of the languages of Kenya). Kenya was taken by the British in the 1880s so that they could control Lake Victoria, the **source** of the Nile River.

Since independence in 1963, Kenya has usually had a one-party government and has been a member of the British Commonwealth. The people are, like the Congo, divided into many tribes who often fight; but Kenya's government has tried to get the people to work together and has encouraged them to run businesses and factories. Kenya is a developing country, slowly growing more modern.

Put a C if the statement is about Congo, K if it is about Kenya, or B for both.

2.53 _____ on the equator

2.54 _____ Congo River

2.55 _____ Joseph Mobutu

2.56 _____ colony of Belgium

2.57 _____ colony of Great Britain

2.58 _____ people come from many different tribes

2.59 _____ savanna

2.60 _____ rainforest

2.61 _____ Swahili culture and language

2.62 _____ riverboats can trade between cities

2.63 _____ Henry Stanley explored it

2.64 _____ east coast city-states traded with Arabs

2.65 _____ famous for its animal safaris

2.66 _____ Lake Victoria

2.67 _____ member of the British Commonwealth of Nations

Review the material in this section to prepare for the Self Test. The Self Test will check your understanding of this section and will review the previous section. Any items you miss on this test will show you what areas you will need to restudy in order to prepare for the unit test.

SELF TEST 2

Match these vocabulary words and definitions (1 point each answer).

2.01	_____ canal	a. the beginning of a river
2.02	_____ harbor	b. person who moves from place to place to find food for himself or his animals
2.03	_____ estuary	c. part of a sea that goes inland to the opening of a river
2.04	_____ ancient	d. able to be traveled on by ships
2.05	_____ refugee	e. a group of related families
2.06	_____ nomad	f. part of a river where it flows into a lake or the ocean
2.07	_____ navigable	g. a person who flees for safety
2.08	_____ clan	h. belonging to times long past
2.09	_____ mouth	i. a deep bay used to shelter ships
2.010	_____ source	j. a waterway dug across land for ships to go through

Each statement is about a country or city. Choose _I_ for Istanbul, _H_ for Hong Kong, _N_ for Nepal, _J_ for Japan, _C_ for D.R. Congo, or _K_ for Kenya (4 points each answer).

2.011 _____ British colony, returned to China in 1997

2.012 _____ archipelago nation, capital Tokyo

2.013 _____ rainforest country on the Congo River

2.014 _____ savanna land, capital Nairobi

2.015 _____ part in Europe, part in Asia

2.016 _____ famous for safaris to see its many wild animals

2.017 _____ in the Himalayas between China and India

2.018 _____ people are Muslim Turks, used to be part of Ottoman Empire

2.019 _____ main religion is Shinto in this crowded, modern country

2.020 _____ main religion is Hinduism, one of the poorest countries on earth

Name the continent for each place (2 points each answer).

2.021 _____ Hong Kong   2.022 _____ London

2.023 _____ Nile River   2.024 _____ Alps

2.025 _____ Nepal   2.026 _____ Gobi Desert

2.027 _____ Japan   2.028 _____ Switzerland

2.029 _____ Sahara Desert   2.030 _____ Ukraine

Choose the correct word to complete each sentence (3 points each answer).

Ukraine	Switzerland	London	Iceland
Kalahari	Columbus	Apollo	*Sputnik*
Suez	Ural		

2.031 _____ was the American space program that landed on the moon.

2.032 _____ is an island settled by Vikings.

2.033 _____ was founded by the Romans on the River Thames.

2.034 _____ is a mountain country famous for its cheese, watches, and chocolate.

2.035 _____ was the first satellite launched into space.

2.036 _____ is a desert in Botswana on the Tropic of Capricorn.

2.037 _____ is a country on the steppes that used to be communist.

2.038 The Isthmus of _____ connects Asia and Africa.

2.039 The _____ Mountains are part of the line that divides Europe and Asia.

2.040 _____ sailed into the West Indies trying to sail west from Europe to Asia.

✔ **Teacher check:**   Initials _____ $\dfrac{80}{100}$

Score _____   Date _____

3. SOUTHERN CONTINENTS

Most of the land and people in the world are in the Northern Hemisphere. But, the three southern continents, Australia, South America, and Antarctica, all have places we studied this year.

This section will review the Australian Desert and the seaport of Sydney on the Island Continent. In South America, the Atacama Desert, the mountain country of Peru, the rainforest of the Amazon in Brazil, and the grassland country of Argentina will be reviewed. Then you will review the frozen continent of Antarctica, the "last place on earth."

Objectives

Read these objectives. When you have completed this section, you should be able to:

1. Describe each of the places you have studied this year in a short statement.
2. Locate each place and feature you have studied on a map and name the continent where it is located.
3. Recognize the meaning of the vocabulary words from the year.
4. Name and locate the continents, oceans, equator, Tropics of Cancer and Capricorn, and the North and South Poles.

Review of Australia

Australia is called the "Land Down Under" because it is under the equator, south of Japan in Asia. It is also called the Island Continent, because it is the smallest of the seven important land masses on earth. It is also the only continent that is all one country!

The center of the continent is a vast desert. Around the edges of the desert are steppes, which are used to raise sheep, one of Australia's most important exports. Because it is in the Southern Hemisphere, the seasons in Australia are reversed, with hot weather coming in December and January.

Australia was claimed for Great Britain by Captain James Cook, who landed on the continent in 1770. Cook was an navy officer on an **expedition** to explore the southern oceans. There was a small **population** of dark-skinned people called Aborigines living in Australia at the time.

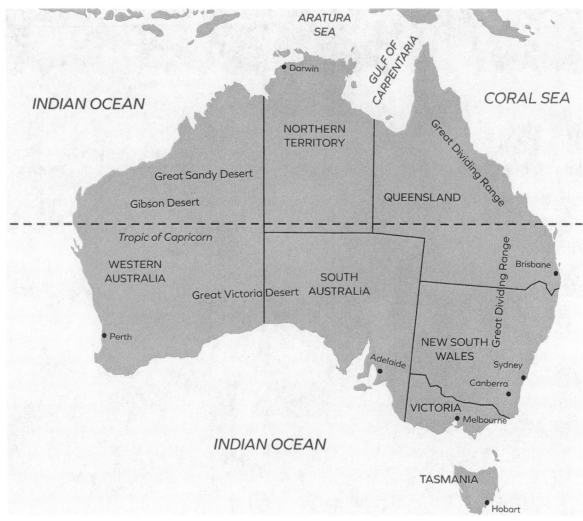

| Australia

HISTORY & GEOGRAPHY 410

LIFEPAC TEST

NAME _____

DATE _____

SCORE _____

HISTORY & GEOGRAPHY 410: LIFEPAC TEST

Choose the correct place from the list below (4 points each answer).

London	Iceland	Ukraine	Switzerland
Istanbul	Nepal	Kenya	Hong Kong
Congo	Japan	Peru	Argentina
Brazil	Sydney	Mexico	Greenland
Canada	West Indies	Cuba	Central America

1. _____ is the largest country in North America, which was claimed by the French for its fur and later taken by the British.

2. _____ is in the Andes Mountains and was the home of the Inca Empire.

3. The Amazon River flows mainly through _____ , and its rainforest was an important source of rubber from 1870 to 1913.

4. _____ is an archipelago nation just east of Korea where the main religion is Shinto and the emperor is from the Yamato clan.

5. _____ was founded by the Romans on the Thames River and is now the home of the British monarch.

6. _____ is a neutral country in the Alps famous for its cheese, watches, and chocolate.

7. _____ is the largest island on earth, and its people are a mix of Inuit and Viking.

8. _____ is a country of mostly European immigrants, that became rich by selling wheat and beef raised on the Pampas to Europe.

9. _____ is an island in the Antilles archipelago whose major exports are sugar and tobacco, and it is still communist.

10. _____ is a region that includes the Isthmus of Panama, Belize, Honduras, and many volcanoes.

11. _____ is a Turkish city in Europe and Asia that was the capital of both the Byzantine and Ottoman Empires.

12. _____ is an island nation settled by Vikings that has very little pollution due to geothermal and hydroelectric power and still uses the Viking Norse language.

13. _____ is a nation whose savanna is poor farmland, but it does produce lions, giraffes, leopards, and cheetahs which people safari to see.

14. _____ 's heartland is the Central Plateau between the Sierra Madre Mountains, where the Spanish conquered the Aztec Indians.

15. _____ is a city in the Southern Hemisphere that began as a British penal colony and became a big exporter of sheep products.

16. _____ includes the islands of Hispaniola, Jamaica, the Bahamas, and Puerto Rico. Its culture is a mix of African and European.

17. _____ is in the rainforest of an African river explored by Henry Stanley and claimed by the king of Belgium.

18. _____ is a crowded Chinese land with a city named Victoria that was a British colony from 1841 until 1997.

19. _____ is a former communist country on the steppes, where Eastern Orthodox Christianity is the largest religion.

20. _____ is in the Himalaya Mountains. Most of its people are Hindu or Buddhist, and the capital is Kathmandu.

Use the clues to name the continent (2 points each answer).

21. _____ Peru, Amazon River, Atacama Desert, most of it is south of the equator

22. _____ Greenland, Isthmus of Panama, Hudson Bay, the Great Lakes, Mississippi River

23. _____ largest continent, Nepal, Gobi Desert, Arabian Desert, Hong Kong

24. _____ Island Continent, Sydney, most of the center is desert, called the Outback

25. _____ South Pole, coldest place on earth, last place on earth to be explored and mapped

26. _____ Alps Mountains, Ukraine, London, its people explored the earth beginning in the 1400s

27. _____ Congo River, Kenya, Sahara Desert, Nile River, Lake Victoria, mostly in the tropics

Write *true* or *false* on the blank (1 point each answer).

28. _____ Christopher Columbus led the first voyage around the world.

29. _____ The United States was the first country to put a man in space.

30. _____ The first man to reach the North Pole was Richard Byrd.

31. _____ During the Age of Exploration, the explorers in the Arctic were looking for the Northwest Passage.

32. _____ Many deserts are found along the equator, which tends to be a dry area.

33. _____ The soil in a rainforest is not very fertile.

Map work.

3.1 What are three names of the Australian Deserts?

_____

3.2 What important map line runs through Australia?

_____

3.3 What is the large island south of Melbourne? _____

Investigate the Mystery!

3.4 The capital of colonial Hong Kong was named Victoria, the largest lake in Africa is named Victoria, and one of the deserts in Australia is also named Victoria! Who is this Victoria, and why were things named after her on three continents? Your assignment, detective, is to find the answer to that question and write a paragraph about it! HINT: Great Britain was the ruler of all three places.

Teacher check:

Initials _____ Date _____

Australian Desert. The desert center of Australia is on the Tropic of Capricorn, and moisture from the Pacific is blocked by the Great Dividing Range. A little water can be found underground, in water holes, or in _playas_, empty lakes that fill up for a little while after a rain. The largest playa is called Lake Disappointment. Sheep can be raised on some of the dry grasslands, but most of the land in the "outback" is empty.

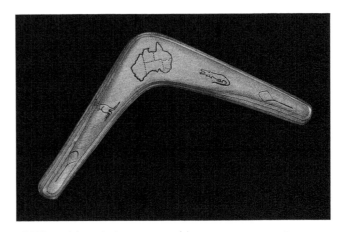

| The Aborigines used boomerangs to hunt; if the prey isn't hit, the boomerang returns to the thrower.

The Aborigines who lived in the desert knew the land well in order to survive there. They were hunter/gatherers. They moved around to find food and could get water from frogs buried in the desert soil when they could not find a water hole.

| Sydney Harbour Bridge

Today the people of Australia use modern machines to live in the desert. The children often go to school by Internet, and doctors come by airplane in an emergency. Air conditioning makes it cooler in the houses. One town, Coober Pedy, is even built underground to help it keep cool!

Sydney. Britain decided to use the land Captain Cook discovered as a **penal colony**. The "First Fleet," the first ships loaded with prisoners, arrived in 1788 and began building the city of Sydney on Port Jackson harbor. The prisoners were given land after they had served their sentences, but very few were ever able to pay for the trip back to Britain. So most of them stayed, and the colony grew.

Sydney and Australia attracted colonists from Britain when it was discovered that sheep raising was very successful there. Several other colonies were founded along the coast, mainly in the east. These colonies formed the Commonwealth of Australia in 1901 and today are an independent member of the British Commonwealth of Nations.

Port Jackson is a huge harbor, with room for thousands of ships. Coal, meat, wheat, and wool are some of the important exports that go out of the port. The harbor itself has two important **landmarks**. The Sydney Harbour Bridge, which links the two sides of the harbor, and the Opera House, with its roof that looks like the sails of a ship, are recognized quickly by visitors.

The people of Sydney are called "Sydneysiders." Their city is very spread out, because all the people want a house with a small yard of their own. The people like to swim at Sydney's many beaches, go "bushwalking" in the nearby national parks, play soccer or cricket, and race boats. The former penal colony has become a rich, important city down under.

Put the correct word in the blank to complete the sentence.

3.5   Because it is south of the equator, Australia is called the Land _____

_____ .

3.6   Australia is called the _____ Continent because it is the smallest of

the seven continents.

3.7   Captain _____ was the British navy officer who

discovered Australia.

3.8   July and August are (what season?) _____ in Australia.

3.9   _____ were the people living in Australia when

Britain took it as a colony.

3.10   _____ are empty lakes that fill up for a short time after a rain.

3.11   Sydney was used by Britain as a _____ colony beginning in 1788.

3.12   Sydney is built on the harbor _____ .

3.13   The two important landmarks of Sydney's harbor are the _____

_____ and the _____ .

3.14   The people of Sydney are called _____ .

Review of South America

South America is in both the Western and Southern Hemispheres, but mostly in the Southern Hemisphere. It is connected to North America by the Isthmus of Panama, which is completely in North America. Both continents were named after Amerigo Vespucci, an Italian explorer who was a part of the earliest voyages to explore and map the New World. Most of the countries of South America were colonies of Spain beginning in the 1500s. Brazil was the one major exception. It was a colony of the country of Portugal, Spain's neighbor in Europe.

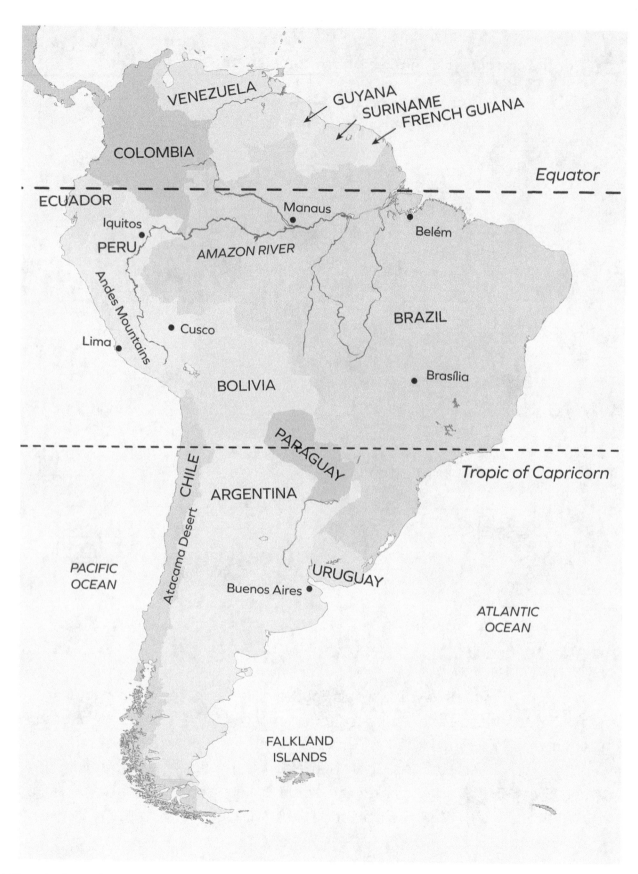

| South America

Map work.

3.15   Circle the capital cities of Buenos Aires, Brasilia, and Lima.

3.16   Name two countries that the equator goes through.

_____

3.17   Name two countries that the Tropic of Capricorn goes through.

_____

3.18   Put a square around the Isthmus of Panama.

3.19   Which part of the continent is bigger, the part north of the equator or the part

to the south? _____

3.20   What country is east of Guyana? _____

Atacama Desert. The Atacama Desert, on the Tropic of Capricorn in Chile, is one of the driest places on earth. In some places less than an inch of rain falls every <u>ten</u> <u>years</u>. Only one of the rivers from the Andes Mountains reaches the ocean through the desert. The rest disappear into the dry soil.

The Atacama is a desert not because mountains block moisture from reaching it, but because the ocean does! The water on the west coast of Chile is very cold, because it has come north from Antarctica. Moisture cannot stay in the cold air above the cold water, so mainly fog reaches the land, but very little rain.

The people of Chile have learned how to get water from the fog to help them live. They "harvest the clouds" by putting up plastic sheets with pans underneath. The fog collects on the plastic and drips into the pans, giving the people water for crops and drinking.

Peru. Peru is a mountain country just north of Chile in the Andes Mountains. It is the source of the Amazon River, which crosses the continent to the Atlantic Ocean. Ships can sail down the Amazon from Iquinto in Peru, all the way to the Atlantic Ocean. That means goods from Peru can go from ports on the Pacific coast or ports on the Amazon in order to reach the Atlantic.

Peru was the home of the Inca Empire. The Incas were a well-organized Indian civilization that began the city of Cuzco (now called Cusco) about 1,000 years before

Jesus was born. Beginning in the 1400s, they conquered many nearby tribes and built an empire in the Andes.

The Inca forced the people to work for the king for a certain number of days every year. They used this "work tax" to build fine roads all over their empire. They also built **terraces** on the sides of the mountains to grow crops, and huge cities with rich palaces for the rulers.

Records were kept on *quipa*, knotted ropes, since the Incas never invented writing. These could be quickly sent anywhere in the empire by a series of relay runners set up along the roads. Heavier loads were sent by llamas, the pack animals of the Andes.

The Incas were rich in gold and silver which could be found in the mountains. The Spanish wanted that treasure when they discovered the nation in the 1500s. Francisco Pizzaro, a Spanish man, kidnapped and killed the Inca ruler in 1532, even after his people paid a huge amount of treasure for his release. The Incas fought the Spanish for many years, but the last Inca king was killed in 1572.

| Inca ceremonial knife

Peru was a Spanish colony until 1821. Spanish is still the main language of the people, although many also speak Quechua, the Inca language. Most of the people belong to the Catholic Church, which is also the church of Spain. The culture of Peru, like much of South America, is a mix of Indian and Spanish, as are the people.

Answer these questions.

3.21   What piece of land connects North and South America?

_____

3.22   What stops moisture from reaching the Atacama Desert? _____

_____

3.23   What does it mean to "harvest the clouds"?_____

_____

3.24 How can ocean ships reach Peru from the Atlantic?_____

_____

3.25 What was the Inca "work tax" used to build?_____

_____

3.26 What were *quipa*? _____

3.27 Why did the Spanish want to conquer the Incas?_____

_____

3.28 What did Francisco Pizzaro do in 1532?_____

_____

3.29 The culture of Peru is a mix of which two cultures?_____

_____

Amazonia. Amazonia is the rainforest around the Amazon River, mostly in the country of Brazil. It is the largest rainforest in the world. The Amazon River is the second longest in the world and carries more water than any other river on earth. It is navigable all the way across the continent to Peru. The river floods every year from December to May, turning miles of forest into lake for a time.

Amazonia was home to many Amerindian (American Indian) tribes for a long time before the Europeans came. Portugal took over Brazil in the 1500s and killed many of the Indians. Those deep in the forest survived because the Europeans could not reach them. Many still live there by hunting and slash-and-burn farming

| Amazon Indian hunter

(burning a small piece of land to farm and leaving when it is no longer fertile).

The Europeans left the forest alone, trading with the Indians for some of the jungle products like Brazil nuts, cocoa, wood, and Amazon fish. One useful product was rubber, taken from the **sap** of an Amazon tree. In 1839, the invention of **vulcanizing** meant rubber no longer got sticky in hot weather and brittle in cold. Many people began to find uses for it, especially for tires for automobiles.

From 1870 until 1913 there was a **boom** in Brazilian rubber. The city of Manuas on the Amazon River became a rich, beautiful city from the trade in rubber. But soon rubber trees were being grown in the rainforest of Asia on plantations that produced the sap more cheaply. Amazonia still produces rubber, but it is no longer as important as it once was.

Brazil has tried to open up the rainforest to settlers. Many of the very poor people of Brazil are going to the forest to start farms for themselves. But the soil of the rainforest is very poor—it only stays fertile by the constant dropping of leaves, branches, and vines that die and fertilize it. When people burn off the forest and farm the land for a few years, then must leave because it no longer produces crops, the forest does not grow back. Only barren land is left. Thus, the settlements are causing more problems than they solve.

Argentina. Argentina is a grassland nation south of Brazil. It is the second-largest country on the continent, after Brazil. The northern part of the country is tropical rainforest, while the southern tip is only 600 miles from Antarctica. In fact, Tierra del Fuego, the island at the southern tip of the country, has become an important place to start visits to Antarctica. Much of the southern part of the nation is a region called Patagonia, a dry, windy plateau of steppes and desert.

Argentina was one of the wealthiest countries in the world in the early 1900s. Its wealth came from the Pampas, the plains around Buenos Aires in the central part of the nation. The Pampas are a rich grassland, where wheat and cattle can be raised. These crops were sold to Europe and made Argentina rich.

| South American gaucho

Argentina's riches were based on crops, so when Europe stopped buying so much during the 1930s, Argentina's great wealth was lost. Ever since that time, bad government has kept the country from doing better. The army has taken over the government many times, and the country is deeply in **debt** because the rulers spent too much.

Argentina is a European country in South America. Most of the people are **descendants** of immigrants from Europe. They came to start new lives as farmers, ranchers, or businessmen in the days when Argentina was so well off.

The people of Argentina speak Spanish, since this was also a Spanish colony. They have cars, TV's, and other things much like the United States. They also have their own culture. They like British tea time, soccer, and all kinds of horseback activities. The gaucho, the cowboy of the Pampas, is an important part of the country's **folklore**. Stories and songs about the gaucho are very popular, even though most of the people live in cities, one third in Buenos Aires alone.

Choose the correct word to complete these sentences.

3.30   The Amazon is the _____ -longest river in the world, and it carries

more _____ than any other.

3.31   An important Amazon product that boomed from 1870 to 1913 was

_____ .

3.32   The Indians of the Amazon live by _____ and _____

farming.

3.33   Argentina's rich grassland is called the _____ .

3.34   _____ is the island on Argentina's southern tip.

3.35   The dry, windy plateau of southern Argentina is called

_____ .

3.36   Most of the people of Argentina are descendants of _____

immigrants.

3.37   The _____ is the cowboy of Argentina and an important part of

their folklore.

Answer these questions.

3.38   What is the problem with Brazil in trying to settle the rainforest?

_____

_____

3.39   Why was Argentina so rich in the early 1900s?

_____

3.40   Two bad things about Argentina's government have kept the country from
doing better. What are they? _____

_____

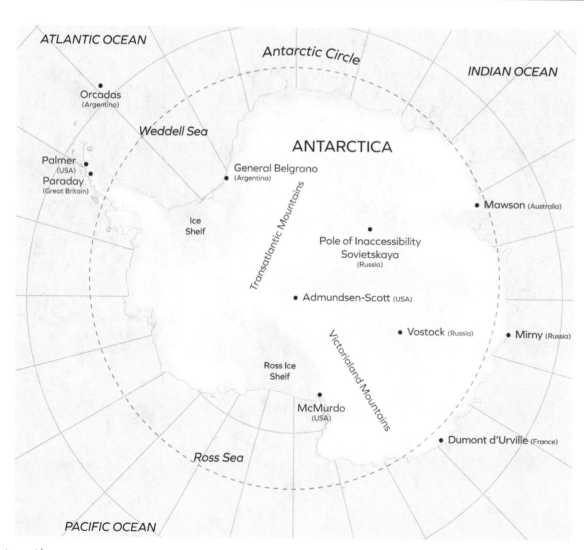

| Antarctica

Review of Antarctica

Antarctica is the continent around the South Pole. It is an icy desert. The air is so cold that it cannot hold much moisture, and it rarely snows there. When it does snow, however, it never melts—it just piles up ice, deeper and deeper. In some places the ice is a mile or more deep! The ice moves slowly out toward the ocean, where it will break off (calve) and form **icebergs**. Antarctica is the coldest place on earth. It is colder than the North Pole because it is higher in **altitude** and, being on land, away from the warming waters of the ocean.

Map work.

3.41   Circle the Antarctic Peninsula.

3.42   The Atlantic, Indian, and Pacific Ocean are all what direction from the South Pole? _____

3.43   What is covering the two large bays on the continent?_____

Our earth is tilted as it orbits the sun. The top and bottom of the earth take turns pointing at or away from the sun. When one is pointed toward the sun, the sun will shine all day and night. At the other end of the world, it will be dark all day and night. The Arctic Circle in the north and the Antarctic Circle in the south mark the areas that receive all-day darkness or light. The polar regions are inside those circles.

Inside the Antarctic Circle is almost all land. It was the last place on earth to be explored and mapped. Well into the 1800s maps of the world were blank around the South Pole. No one knew what was there. Gradually daring explorers risked the icebergs to find out.

Captain James Cook, who discovered Australia, was one of the earliest explorers. He sailed as far south as he dared in 1772, and became the first person to cross the Antarctic Circle. Many men followed Cook to hunt the whales and seals he saw in the area. Other explorers also followed. When they found land, they named it and put it on a map. Gradually, they learned the location of the land and islands in the south.

By the middle of the 1800s, the explorers were fairly sure that there was a large continent around the South Pole. Most of the exploration had been by boats until then. Now the men began to stay through the winter and explore the land.

The first people to stay all winter stayed in ships frozen in the ocean ice beginning in the 1890s. As soon as the sun returned after the time of darkness, they would explore and map. The cold, blizzards, and the long hours of darkness made the winters very difficult.

| McMurdo station, Antarctica

Many of the explorers wanted to reach the South Pole. There was a race to see who could get their first. In 1911 two teams set off across the Ross Ice Shelf, the place where ships could get the closest to the Pole. The team led by Roald Amundsen of Norway won, reaching the pole on December 14, 1911. Through better planning, he beat the team led by Robert Scott of Britain by five weeks. Scott and his team reached the pole, but they all died on the way back.

In 1929 Admiral Richard Byrd was the first man to fly an airplane over the South Pole. He also led several expeditions to explore the continent. With the help of airplanes, most of the continent was finally mapped by about 1958.

There are no land animals in Antarctica, because there are no plants there for them to eat. Seals and penguins are sea animals who visit the land. They often eat krill, small shrimp-like animals that live in the ocean around the continent.

Antarctica is too cold for people to make a home there. Several countries, including the United States, have research stations in Antarctica where scientists live and work for short periods of time. Some of these stations have people in them all year. The countries of the world have agreed to share Antarctica and use it only for science. So far, that agreement seems to be working well.

Match these people.

3.44 _____ James Cook

3.45 _____ Roald Amundsen

3.46 _____ Robert Scott

3.47 _____ Richard Byrd

a. led second team to South Pole, died on the way back

b. first to cross Antarctic Circle

c. first to fly plane over South Pole

d. led first team to South Pole

Write *true* or *false* on the blank.

3.48 _____ Antarctica is an icy desert.

3.49 _____ The North Pole is colder than the South Pole.

3.50 _____ Antarctica is the only place on earth where the sun can shine all day and night.

3.51 _____ The first people to stay all winter in Antarctica did it in camps on the ice shelves.

3.52 _____ Most of Antarctica was finally mapped by 1958.

3.53 _____ There are several kinds of small land animals in Antarctica.

3.54 _____ Antarctica is open to all countries who want to do scientific work there.

Review the material in this section to prepare for the Self Test. The Self Test will check your understanding of this section and will review the other sections. Any items you miss on this test will show you what areas you will need to restudy in order to prepare for the unit test.

SELF TEST 3

Each statement is about a place studied in this section. Put an *S* for Sydney, *P* for Peru, *B* for Brazil, *Arg* for Argentina, and *Ant* for Antarctica (4 points each answer).

3.01 _____ Port Jackson

3.02 _____ coldest place on earth

3.03 _____ Amazon River

3.04 _____ Inca Empire

3.05 _____ in the Andes Mountains

3.06 _____ the Pampas

3.07 _____ the rainforest had a boom in rubber from 1870 to 1913

3.08 _____ one of the richest countries on earth in the early 1900s

3.09 _____ country made up mostly of immigrants from Europe

3.010 _____ European colony began as a penal colony

3.011 _____ South Pole

3.012 _____ colony became successful by raising sheep

3.013 _____ on the "Island Continent"

3.014 _____ colony of Portugal in South America

3.015 _____ was not finally mapped until about 1958

Name the continent for each place (2 points each answer).

3.016 _____ Ukraine   3.017 _____ Nepal

3.018 _____ Iceland   3.019 _____ Kenya

3.020 _____ Peru   3.021 _____ London

3.022 _____ Congo River   3.023 _____ Hong Kong

3.024 _____ Kalahari Desert   3.025 _____ Gobi Desert

Write *true* or *false* on the blank (each answer, 1 point).

3.026 _____ A penal colony is a settlement in another country for the purpose of punishing lawbreakers.

3.027 _____ Australia and Kenya are part of the British Commonwealth.

3.028 _____ Most of the center of Australia is desert.

3.029 _____ *Sputnik* was the American space program that landed on the moon.

3.030 _____ Japan is an archipelago nation in Asia.

3.031 _____ Switzerland is a country in the Himalaya Mountains in Asia.

3.032 _____ Iceland is an island that was settled by Vikings.

3.033 _____ The grassland of Kenya is savanna.

3.034 _____ Prince Henry was the English explorer who first crossed the Antarctic Circle.

3.035 _____ More people live in the Southern Hemisphere because it has more land than the Northern.

3.036 _____ Altitude is owing something to another, often money.

3.037 _____ The Incas used knotted ropes called *quipa* to make records.

3.038 _____ Rainforest land is not very fertile.

3.039 _____ South America is in the Western Hemisphere.

3.040 _____ The Atacama Desert is dry because of the cold water coming up from Antarctica along the coast of Chile.

3.041 _____ The Inca Empire was rich in gold and silver.

3.042 _____ Ukraine, Argentina, and Istanbul are rich grassland countries.

3.043 _____ There are no land animals in Antarctica.

3.044 _____ Christianity is the main religion in Nepal.

3.045 _____ Hong Kong was a British colony which is now part of Brazil.

Teacher check:

Score _____

Initials _____

Date _____

80 / 100

4. NORTH AMERICA, NORTH POLE

North America is the one continent you studied by itself this year. This section will review the features of this continent. It will also review Greenland, Canada, the United States, Mexico, Central America, and the West Indies, which includes the island nation of Cuba. Then this section will review the region around the North Pole, so similar and yet so different from Antarctica.

Objectives

Read these objectives. When you have completed this section, you should be able to:

1. Describe each of the places you have studied this year in a short statement.
2. Locate each place and feature you have studied on a map and name the continent where it is located.
3. Recognize the meaning of the vocabulary words from the year.
4. Name and locate the continents, oceans, equator, Tropics of Cancer and Capricorn, and the North and South Poles.

Review of North America

North America is the third-largest continent on earth (after Asia and Africa). It has mountains running all the way down its western side from Alaska to Panama. There are also mountains, the Appalachians, along the east coast of the United States. Between these two mountain ranges is a huge plain that includes the Great Plains, a rich grass-land region. In the north, around Hudson Bay, is the Canadian Shield, a rocky plateau rich in minerals.

The northern part of the continent is tundra, inside the Arctic Circle of the polar region. The southern end, in Central America, is tropical rainforest. Clearly, the North American continent covers a wide range of climates.

The first people in America were Asians who crossed the Bering Strait. They became the Native American or Indian tribes of the continent. After the Age of Exploration, Europeans began to conquer the land and immigrate there. The better machines and greater numbers of Europeans helped them to conquer the Indians. Europeans become the largest group on the continent. U.S. and Canadian culture is mostly European, while Mexico and Central America are a mix of Spanish and Indian. The West Indies is a mix of European and African.

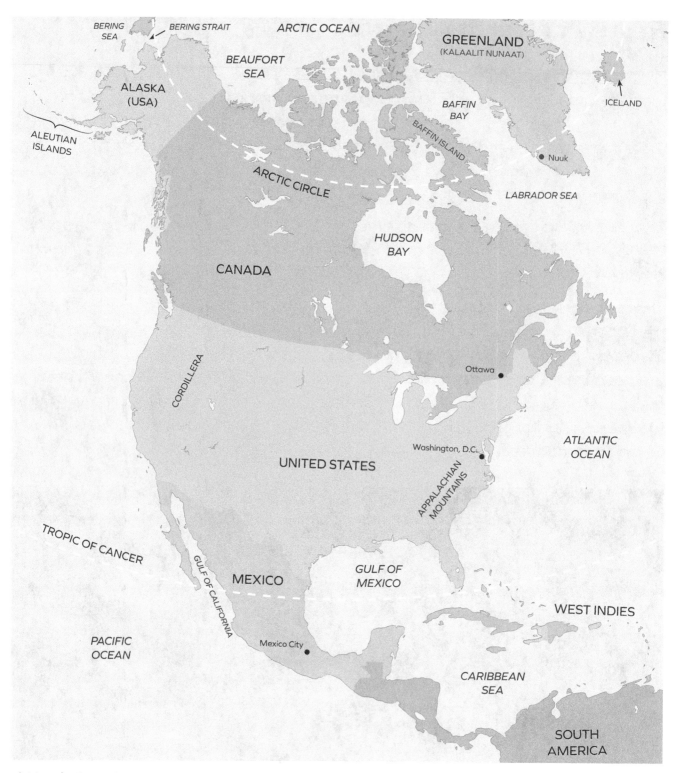

| North America

Map work. Use an atlas if you need help.

4.1   Circle the Great Lakes and the Aleutian Islands on the map.

4.2   Draw in the Mississippi River.

4.3   Shade in the countries of Central America.

4.4   The Gulf of Mexico and the Caribbean Sea are part of the

_____ Ocean.

4.5   Underline the capital cities of Greenland (Kalaallit Nunaat) Canada, the U.S.,

and Mexico.

Greenland. Greenland (Kalaallit Nunaat) is the largest island in the world and a colony of Denmark. The island is mainly north of the Arctic Circle and is covered by a thick ice cap all year around. The northernmost piece of land in the world is Point Morris Jesup in Greenland. The people are a mix of Inuit (Native American) and Vikings who colonized the island from Iceland in about A.D. 981. They live mainly in the ice-free areas along the coast.

Canada. Canada is the largest country in North America and the second largest in the world. It is a wealthy country, rich in mineral resources, fertile land, and factories. It is not crowded; large parts of the country are **uninhabited**. Most of the people live in the warmer south, near the U.S. border.

Canada was claimed and settled by France in the 1500-1600s. The French were mainly interested in the fur trade, because Europeans paid good prices for furs at that time. France lost its colonies to Britain after several wars in the 1600s and 1700s. British colonists then began to settle on the land, too. Because of this Canada has both a French and British **heritage**.

| Cross-country skiing is popular in the snow environments

Canada never fought Britain for its independence like the United States. Instead, the colonies were slowly given more and more self-government. They formed the Dominion of Canada in 1867. Today Canada is an independent member of the British Commonwealth. The country is a **federation** of ten provinces and two territories (as of 1997). Each province has its own government, as well as the national government in Ottawa.

Circle the correct word to complete the sentence.

4.6   North America is the (second / third) -largest continent.

4.7   The (Canadian Shield / Appalachian Highland) is a rocky plateau, rich in minerals, around Hudson Bay.

4.8   (Europeans / Asians) are the largest group on the continent.

4.9   Indians are descendants of Asians who came to America across the (Bering Strait / Caribbean Sea).

4.10   (Greenland / Cuba) is the largest island on earth.

4.11   The northernmost point of land on earth is in (Canada / Greenland).

4.12   Most of Greenland is covered by (tundra / an ice cap).

4.13   The European ancestors of the Greenlanders were (British / Viking).

4.14   Canada is the (fourth / second)-largest nation in the world.

4.15   Canada has both a French and a (British / Spanish) heritage.

4.16   France was interested in Canada for the (wool / fur) trade.

4.17   Canada (never did / did) fight for its independence.

4.18   Most of the people in Canada live in the (west / south).

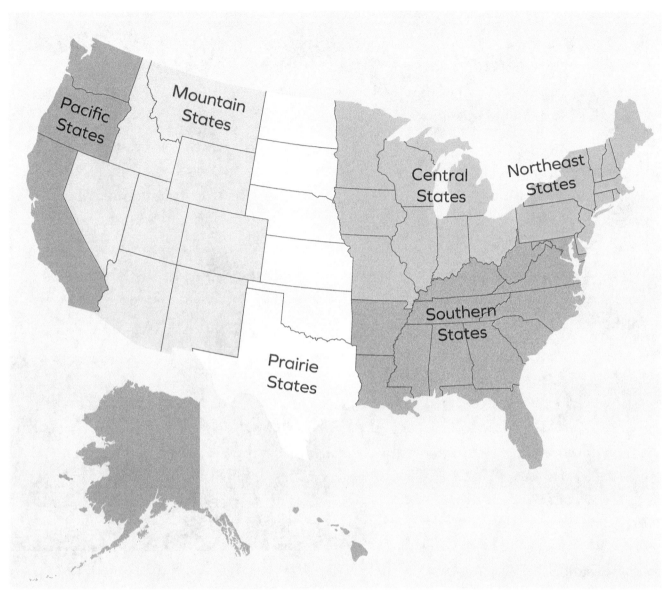

| Regions of the United States

United States. The United States is the most powerful country on earth. It is a federation of fifty states. Forty-eight of these are **contiguous** states located in the center of North America. The people of America immigrated from many different countries all over the world, but mainly from Europe. It is an English-speaking nation, with a culture that honors hard work and independence.

The Northeastern States are mountainous, with poor, rocky soil. The fast-moving rivers of these states were used to produce power for the country's first factories. This region was important in American history as the heartland of the country when it rebelled against Britain. Much of the Revolutionary War was fought here.

The Southern States tried in the 1860s to make their own country called the Confederacy, so they could keep their black slaves. Eventually, after four years of civil war, they were forced to end slavery and stay in the United States. The American capital, Washington, District of Columbia, is here. The Coastal Plains of this region are fine farmlands, with rivers to ship crops and goods.

The Central States are on the St. Lawrence Seaway. The Seaway uses rivers, canals, and lakes to connect the Great Lakes to the Atlantic Ocean. This gives the U.S. and Canada port cities that are far inland. Goods from this region can also be sent down the Mississippi River to the Gulf of Mexico. Thus, the fertile farmland has two easy ways to ship out crops.

The Prairie States are on the Great Plains, America's rich grassland. The land is used to raise grain and cattle. It was some of the last land settled in America because it was so dry that people believed it was a desert.

The Mountain States are in the **Cordillera**, America's largest mountain chain. The mountains block moisture from reaching the Great Basin Desert located up in the highlands. Most of this region is dry, but it has some beautiful scenery, such as the Grand Canyon. The Great Salt Lake in Utah is in the Great Basin. Water can come in but cannot get out, so it evaporates, leaving salt behind.

| America's Mt. St. Helens erupted in 1980.

The Pacific States include Alaska and Hawaii which are not part of the contiguous states. Hawaii is an archipelago of volcanoes, some still active, in the Pacific Ocean. Alaska and the other states of this region are in the Cordillera and are located on **faults** that cause earthquakes. Volcanoes, like Mount St. Helens that erupted in 1980, can also be active in this region.

American Southwest Desert. The American Southwest Desert covers much of the southern part of the Pacific and Mountain States, as well as northern Mexico. It includes the Great Basin and several other deserts. The lowest spot in North America, Death Valley (492 feet below sea level), is there.

Match the following regions with the description.

4.19	_____	poor soil, first factories	a. Contiguous States
4.20	_____	Confederacy, Coastal Plains	b. Northeastern
4.21	_____	earthquakes and volcanoes	c. Southern
4.22	_____	Cordillera states, Grand Canyon	d. Central
			e. Prairie
4.23	_____	48 states together in central North America	f. Mountains
			g. Pacific
4.24	_____	Great Plains, last place settled	h. American Southwest Desert
4.25	_____	Great Lakes and Mississippi for shipping goods	
4.26	_____	covers southwest U.S. and northern Mexico	

Mexico. Mexico is covered by the Cordillera. The heartland of Mexico is on the Central Plateau in between the **ranges** of the Sierra Madre Mountains. It is a dry land and not very fertile. Farms are small and often grow only enough to feed one family. But Mexico is rich in mineral resources. It is the world's largest producer of silver, and a leader in oil as well.

Mexico was home to both the Aztec and Maya Indian civilizations before the Europeans came. The Mayas died out before 1500, and the Aztecs were conquered by Spain, which claimed Mexico and most of Central America. Mexico was a Spanish colony until 1821.

Most of the people of Mexico are a mix of Spanish and Indian. They are usually poor. The government is trying to encourage new businesses to give the people jobs and use the country's rich resources in a fairer way.

Central America. Central America consists of the countries of Belize, El Salvador, Guatemala, Honduras, Nicaragua, Costa Rica, and Panama on the southern end of the continent. Here the Isthmus of Panama connects North and South America. It is a mountainous land in the Cordillera. There are many active volcanoes that make the soil on the Pacific side fertile with their ash. The lowlands near the Atlantic are usually rainforest, which is poor soil for farming.

This is another part of the continent where the Maya Indians built great cities long before the Europeans came. All the countries except Belize became Spanish colonies after that. Belize was a colony of Britain. Today most of these countries are very poor, with governments that often are taken over by the military. The people and culture are a mix of Spanish and Indian.

Write *true* or *false* on the blank.

4.27 _____ The heartland of Mexico is on the Coastal Plains of the Gulf of Mexico.

4.28 _____ Mexico was home to the Inca and Maya civilizations.

4.29 _____ The people and cultures of Mexico and Central America are mainly a mix of Spanish and Indian.

4.30 _____ Central America is mainly a flat plain of rainforests and savanna.

4.31 _____ All of the countries of Central America were Spanish colonies.

4.32 _____ There are many volcanoes in Central America which help make the soil on the Pacific side fertile.

List the countries of Central America.

4.33 _____

_____

_____

_____

West Indies. The West Indies includes two archipelagoes, the Antilles and the Bahamas. The Antilles are divided into the Greater Antilles, the larger islands in the north, and the Lesser Antilles, the smaller islands to the south. They were named the Indies by Columbus, who mistakenly thought he was near India when he found them.

| Cuban buildings show Spanish influence.

There are thousands of islands in the West Indies, divided into twenty-four countries. They were, and some still are, colonies of many different nations, including the United States. Tourism is one of the few ways to make money for these tropical islands. They have few factories and most people farm to get their food.

The European nations colonized the islands to set up plantations for crops such as sugar cane that grew well in the climate. They brought in slaves from Africa to do the work, after the Indians on the island died of disease and mistreatment. The culture of the islands today is a mix of European and African, called *Creole*.

The Bahamas are one nation. They are part of the British Common wealth, as is Jamaica, and one of the four main islands of the Greater Antilles. The other three are Hispaniola (divided into the French-speaking countries of Haiti and the Dominican Republic), Puerto Rico (a colony of the United States), and Cuba (a communist nation). Thus, the West Indies show the differences of the many countries that ruled there.

Cuba. Cuba is the largest island in the West Indies and is called the "Pearl of the Antilles." It is mainly gentle hills or plains that are fertile farmland. Sugar and tobacco are the most important crops. Cuba has many mineral resources and several good harbors, including Havana, the capital.

The island was a Spanish colony until the Spanish-American War in 1898. America won the war, and Cuban independence was part of the **treaty** afterward; but Americans kept some control over the Cuban government and businesses. Eventually, Fulgencio Battista, a dictator, took control of the island and was himself thrown out by a communist dictator, Fidel Castro in 1959.

Cuba is one of the few countries in the world that is still communist as of 2015. The island received a great deal of money from the Soviet Union during the time that it was a communist country (1917-1991). Communist governments usually cannot get everything their people need, but things got even worse in Cuba without the Soviet money.

Under communism, the people of Cuba are not allowed to disagree with the government. They must especially say only good things about the dictator. Like many communist dictators, he expects the people to think everything he says and does is wonderful. They can be sent to jail for not agreeing with him. People can also be sent to jail for believing in Jesus. The government controls what the people are allowed to read and often lies about how good life is in Cuba. Life under communism is hard, but the Cuban people still love their beautiful island home.

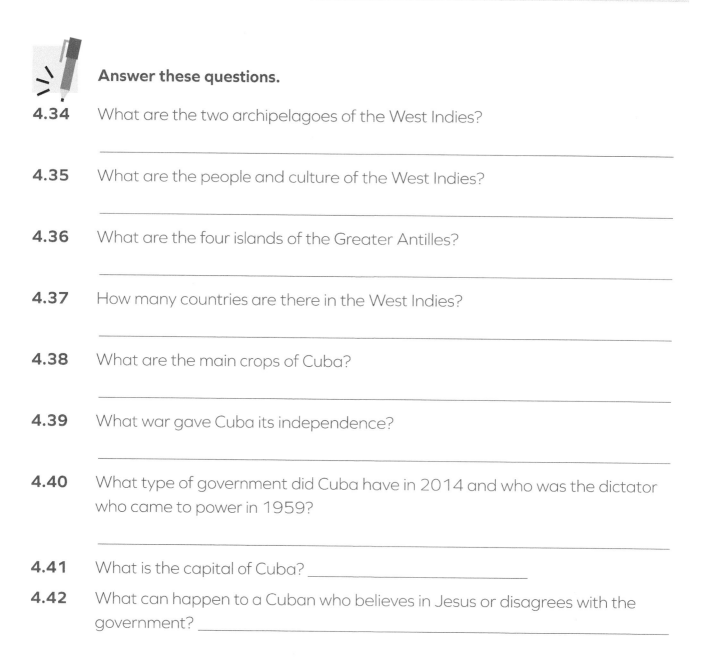

Answer these questions.

4.34   What are the two archipelagoes of the West Indies?

_____

4.35   What are the people and culture of the West Indies?

_____

4.36   What are the four islands of the Greater Antilles?

_____

4.37   How many countries are there in the West Indies?

_____

4.38   What are the main crops of Cuba?

_____

4.39   What war gave Cuba its independence?

_____

4.40   What type of government did Cuba have in 2014 and who was the dictator who came to power in 1959?

_____

4.41   What is the capital of Cuba? _____

4.42   What can happen to a Cuban who believes in Jesus or disagrees with the government? _____

Review of the North Polar Region

The North Pole is not on land, but in the middle of a frozen ocean. Within the Arctic Circle though, are the northern parts of Europe, Asia, and North America; so while people had to make a dangerous ocean voyage to reach the Antarctic Circle, they could just walk to the Arctic!

People have lived there for thousands of years. They live on the land around the edges of the Arctic, however, not on the ice near the Pole. It took a well-organized expedition to reach the North Pole over the "land" created by the frozen pack ice.

The land around the Arctic is usually tundra. Some of the land, like Greenland, is covered with ice caps, or **glaciers** that do not melt, but most arctic land has a short summer when the snow melts and the ground thaws. During the summer **lichens** and flowers grow, small rodents gather food, birds nest, and the animals get fat to be ready for the cold winter. The tundra plants feed animals like musk oxen, reindeer, caribou, lemmings, and Arctic hares. These are eaten by wolves and foxes. The largest meat eater of the Arctic is the polar bear, who lives mainly on the ice, eating seals.

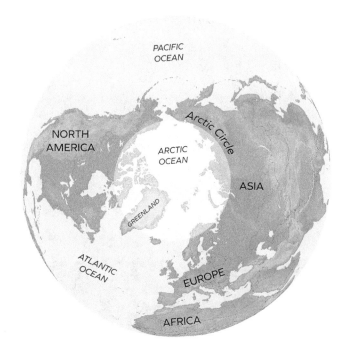

| The North Polar Region

The Lapps (Sami) and Eskimo (Inuit) lived in the Arctic before modern inventions made life there more comfortable. The Lapps of Europe were nomads who herded reindeer. The animals supplied the Lapps with all they needed for food and clothes. The Inuit who lived in Asia and North America were hunter/gatherers. They hunted seals and caribou. The only animals they kept were the dogs which they used to pull their sleds. They would gather berries and roots during the short summers.

During the Age of Exploration, the Europeans explored the Arctic looking for the Northwest Passage. They wanted to find a way around North America to get to the spices of Asia. Henry Hudson made four trips searching for the passage in the 1600s.

He found and named the large bay in Canada after himself. Sir John Franklin tried to find the Passage in 1845 and disappeared. Explorers learned a lot about the Arctic during the long search to find him. Eventually, Roald Amundsen succeeded in sailing through the Passage in 1906, five years before he reached the South Pole.

As was true of the South Pole, there were also many explorers who wanted to be the first to reach the North Pole. The man who did it was Robert E. Peary of the United States. He, his African-American assistant, Matthew Henson, and four Eskimos reached the Pole in 1909. Amundsen heard about it and changed his own plans to go to the North Pole. He went south instead.

American Admiral Richard Byrd was the first man to fly a plane over the North Pole in 1925, and later would also be the first over the South Pole. An American submarine, the U.S.S. *Nautilus*, was the first ship to reach the Pole, going under the ice in 1958! Today men live in the Arctic Circle using snowmobiles, rifles, airplanes, and heaters to make life more comfortable. But the ice of the frozen Arctic Ocean is still the land of explorers and adventurers.

| A submarine punches through the ice

Put in the correct word(s) to complete each sentence.

4.43   The _____ Pole is on the frozen Arctic Ocean.

4.44   The _____ Circle crosses the continents of Europe, Asia, and

_____ .

4.45   The land around the Arctic is usually _____ .

4.46   The _____ are the reindeer-herding nomads of the European

Arctic.

4.47   The Inuit (Eskimos) are the hunter/gatherers of the Arctic on

the continents of _____ and _____ .

4.48   The Arctic explorers of the Age of Exploration were searching for the

_____ Passage, but the first man to sail through it was

_____ in 1906.

4.49   The first man to reach the North Pole was _____ .

4.50   _____ was the first man to fly over the North Pole,

and the _____ was the first ship to reach it.

Before you take this last Self Test, you may want to do one or more of these self checks.

1.   _____   Read the objectives. See if you can do them.

2.   _____   Restudy the material related to any objectives that you cannot do.

3.   _____   Use the **SQ3R** study procedure to review the material:

    a.   **S**can the sections.

    b.   **Q**uestion yourself.

    c.   **R**ead to answer your questions.

    d.   **R**ecite the answers to yourself.

    e.   **R**eview areas you did not understand.

4.   _____   Review all vocabulary, activities, and Self Tests, writing a correct answer
for every wrong answer.

Crossword Review

 Find the capitals of these places.

Across

2. Congo
4. Ukraine
5. Brazil
8. Argentina
10. Cuba
13. Hong Kong (former capital)
15. Mexico
16. Great Britain (United Kingdom)

Down

1. Kenya
2. Nepal
3. Greenland
6. United States
7. Iceland
9. Canada
11. Peru
12. Switzerland
14. Japan

SELF TEST 4

Name the country for each item. Use *G* for Greenland, *Can* for Canada, *US* for the United States, *M* for Mexico, *CA* for Central America, *WI* for the West Indies, and *Cuba* for Cuba (2 points each answer).

4.01   _____   largest island in the Antilles archipelago

4.02   _____   the heartland is the Central Plateau in between the Sierra Madre Mountains

4.03   _____   includes Belize, Honduras, and El Salvador

4.04   _____   the Isthmus of Panama is here

4.05   _____   largest island in the world

4.06   _____   Bahamas, Hispaniola, and Puerto Rico

4.07   _____   Spain conquered the Aztec civilization here

4.08   _____   has a French and English heritage

4.09   _____   the St. Lawrence Seaway and the Mississippi River give access to Atlantic ports

4.010   _____   Great Plains, Great Basin Desert, and Grand Canyon

4.011   _____   largest country in North America

4.012   _____   people are a mix of Viking and Inuit

4.013   _____   Costa Rica, Guatemala, and Nicaragua

4.014   _____   communist country

4.015   _____   became independent after the Spanish-American War

Answer these questions.

4.016   The Arctic Circle crosses which three continents? (6 points)

_____

4.017   The Canadian Shield is around what large bay? (2 points)

_____

4.018   Early Arctic explorers were looking for a northern way around the New World to Asia that was called what? (2 points)

_____

Match the following (3 point each answer).

4.019 _____ Maya

4.020 _____ Fidel Castro

4.021 _____ Lapps

4.022 _____ Inuit

4.023 _____ Robert Peary

4.024 _____ Richard Byrd

4.025 _____ Roald Amundsen

4.026 _____ Magellan

4.027 _____ Prince Henry

4.028 _____ Apollo

a.   led first voyage around the world

b.   Arctic hunter/gatherers, keep dogs to pull sleds

c.   Mexican and Central American Indian civilization

d.   first man to the North Pole

e.   first man to the South Pole

f.   program that put first person on the moon

g.   first dictator of Cuba

h.   first man to fly over both Poles

i.   led Portuguese effort to reach Asia around Africa

j.   Arctic nomads, herd reindeer

Choose the correct place from the list below (3 points each answer).

Iceland	Istanbul	Sydney	Hong Kong
London	Ukraine	Japan	Peru
Nepal	Kenya		

4.029 _____ is the capital city of Great Britain, founded by the Romans on the Thames River.

4.030 _____ is a country on the fertile European steppes that used to be part of the communist Union of Soviet Socialist Republics.

4.031 _____ is an Asian archipelago nation whose main islands are Honshu, Hokkaido, Kyushu, and Shikoku.

4.032 _____ is a poor nation in the Himalaya Mountains where the main religion is Hinduism.

4.033 _____ is an Australian city where the First Fleet landed to begin a British penal colony.

4.034 _____ is an African savanna country famous for offering safaris to see its many wild animals.

4.035 _____ was a British colony that was returned to China in 1997, even though many of its people were refugees from communist China.

4.036 _____ is a Turkish city in both Europe and Asia that was once Constantinople, the capital of the Byzantine Empire.

4.037 _____ is in the Andes Mountains of South America and was the home of the Inca Empire.

4.038 _____ is a European island nation that has many volcanoes and hot springs and was settled by the Vikings.

Teacher check: Initials _____

Score _____ Date _____

80/100

Before you take the LIFEPAC Test, you may want to do one or more of these self checks.

1. _____ Read the objectives. See if you can do them.

2. _____ Restudy the material related to any objectives that you cannot do.

3. _____ Use the **SQ3R** study procedure to review the material.

4. _____ Review activities, Self Tests, and LIFEPAC vocabulary words.

5. _____ Restudy areas of weakness indicated by the last Self Test.

NOTES

NOTES

NOTES

NOTES